P9-EAJ-177

Mysterious Encounters

Miracles

by Toney Allman

KIDHAVEN PRESS
A part of Gale, Cengage Learning

GALE
CENGAGE Learning

Detroit • New York • San Francisco • New Haven, Conn • Waterville, Maine • London

© 2008 Gale, Cengage Learning

ALL RIGHTS RESERVED. No part of this work covered by the copyright herein may be reproduced, transmitted, stored, or used in any form or by any means graphic, electronic, or mechanical, including but not limited to photocopying, recording, scanning, digitizing, taping, Web distribution, information networks, or information storage and retrieval systems, except as permitted under Section 107 or 108 of the 1976 United States Copyright Act, without the prior written permission of the publisher.

Every effort has been made to trace the owners of copyrighted material.

LIBRARY OF CONGRESS CATALOGING-IN-PUBLICATION DATA

Allman, Toney.
  Miracles / by Toney Allman.
    p. cm. — (Mysterious encounters)
  Includes bibliographical references and index.
  ISBN 978-0-7377-4087-5 (hardcover)
  1. Supernatural—Juvenile literature. 2. Miracles—Juvenile literature.
I. Title.
  BL100.A45 2009
  202'.117—dc22

                                                              2008017840

KidHaven Press
27500 Drake Rd.
Farmington Hills, MI 48331

ISBN-13: 978-0-7377-4087-5
ISBN-10: 0-7377-4087-6

Printed in the United States of America
1 2 3 4 5 6 7 12 11 10 09 08

Contents

Chapter 1

Chapter 2

Chapter 3

Chapter 4

Chapter 1

Do You Believe in Miracles?

Bernadette Soubirous lived in the village of Lourdes, France, beside the Gave de Pau River. In 1858 she was fourteen years old and lived with her desperately poor family in a tiny hut. She was poorly educated because she had to work to help her family survive instead of going to school. No one thought there was anything special about her or her family. One cold February day Bernadette went searching for firewood with her sister and a friend. The girls waded across the Gave de Pau River and went to a little cave, or grotto, on the river's edge. The river waters sometimes swirled into the grotto and washed up wood sticks and other trash there. It was a dark, muddy place that

In 1858 Bernadette Soubirous experienced a miracle when the Virgin Mary appeared to her in a grotto in Lourdes, France.

local people had named the "pigsty" because people used it as a watering hole for their pigs. Here it was that Bernadette experienced a miracle.

A Vision in the Pigsty

Later, Bernadette wrote a description of what happened to her:

As I raised my head to look at the grotto, I saw a Lady dressed in white, wearing a white dress, a blue girdle and a yellow rose on each foot, the same color as the chain of her rosary; the beads of the rosary were white.

The Lady made a sign for me to approach; but I was seized with fear, and I did not dare, thinking that I was faced with an **illusion**. I rubbed my eyes, but in vain. I looked again, and I could still see the same Lady. Then I put my hand into my pocket, and took my rosary. I wanted to make the sign of the cross, but in vain; I could not raise my hand to my forehead, it kept on

Thinking About Visions

Visions of Mary have been reported around the world, usually by young people. Miriam Lambouras is an Orthodox Christian and a disbeliever in these visions. She says, "It is well known that children . . . love to have a secret world inaccessible to adults and often play out in their minds situations where they can be important." She says the visions are vivid imaginings.

Miriam Lambouras, "The Marian Apparitions: Divine Intervention or Delusion?" Orthodox Christian Information Center. www.orthodoxinfo.com/inquirers/marian_apparitions.aspx.

dropping. Then a violent impression took hold of me more strongly, but I did not go.

The Lady took the rosary that she held in her hands and she made the sign of the cross. Then I commenced not to be afraid. I took my rosary again; I was able to make the sign of the cross; from that moment I felt perfectly undisturbed in mind. I knelt down and said my rosary, seeing this Lady always before my eyes. The Vision slipped the beads of her rosary between her fingers, but she did not move her lips. When I had said my rosary the Lady made a sign for me to approach, but I did not dare. I stayed in the same place. Then, all of a sudden, she disappeared.[1]

What Did It Mean?

Bernadette did not understand her vision. She asked her friends if they had seen anything, but they had not. She felt mixed up and frightened, but she admitted to her friends that she had had a vision of a beautiful lady. The other girls promised not to tell anyone of the strange experience, but they could not keep the secret. Soon word of the vision spread throughout the village, and Bernadette's mother told her to stay away from the grotto. She was scared for her daughter, and many villagers thought Bernadette was a liar or crazy.

Bernadette could not stay away from the grotto. Over the next six months, she returned, feeling that the lady wanted her to come. And she kept seeing the beautiful lady. The lady always smiled a lovely

Bernadette Soubirous returned many times to the grotto to see the vision of the Virgin Mary.

smile, and sometimes she spoke to Bernadette. She told Bernadette to pray for sinners. She told her to tell the priests to build a chapel at the grotto. Finally, she directed Bernadette to dig in the earth of the grotto, and a spring bubbled up at that spot. Bernadette visited the grotto eighteen times and was always filled with peace and joy. During one of her last visits, the lady finally gave Bernadette a hint of who she was. She said, "I am the Immaculate Conception."[2] This is a term that the Catholic Church uses for the Virgin Mary, the mother of Jesus.

People in the village and all around France heard of Bernadette's visions and came to the grotto to watch her have the visions and to pray.

Once Bernadette's vision was declared to be a true miracle many people visited the grotto to experience the miracle for themselves, though only Bernadette herself could see the Virgin Mary.

Natural Miracles

Saint Augustine, an ancient philosopher, said, "Miracles are not contrary to nature, but only contrary to what we know about nature."

Quoted in Proverbia.net, "Miracles." http://en.proverbia.net/citastema. asp?tematica=768.

These crowds believed that Bernadette's visions were real. They believed they were watching a true miracle, even though they could see nothing. But authorities and church officials did not believe at first. They were angry and tried to prove that Bernadette was crazy or fooling people on purpose. She was just causing trouble. They questioned Bernadette for many hours and insisted that the miracle was impossible. They tried to prove that the visions were not real, but finally, even the **skeptics** were convinced. Bernadette had used words that she could not have known, such as "Immaculate Conception." In the grotto, she had held a burning candle till the flame licked her hand and had not been burned. After a long investigation, the Catholic Church declared that Bernadette had experienced a miracle. In 1862 the bishop in charge of the investigation reported, "We judge that Mary Immaculate, mother of God, really appeared to Bernadette."[3]

Belief and Disbelief

Even today, many people believe that Bernadette's visions were true miracles from God. They believe that something wonderful happened to Bernadette those long years ago. That is what *miracle* means— something wonderful. Around the world, every religion has a history of miracles, and millions of people believe miracles can happen. In the United States one poll found that 84 percent of Americans believe in miracles. Miracles are religious experiences that come from God or the gods or a supernatural power. Miracles seem to go against the rules of nature. Science cannot explain them. They are the divine way that people are helped when no help in the real world seems possible. They are messages to people that come from outside the natural world. They are rare events that bring something good and unexpected to the people who experience them.

Many people, however, do not believe in miracles that defy the laws of nature. In science there is always more to learn. Perhaps, say these people, miracles are just events that science does not yet understand. Perhaps they could be explained if scientists completely understood all the laws of nature. Perhaps they are coincidences or **hallucinations** (imagined visions). Most scientists do not believe in miracles. P.M. Bhargarva is a scientist who rejects miracles. He says, "Miracles constitute an important part . . . of every religion and a miracle is a miracle only if it cannot be explained

Two Roman soldiers witness the stone being rolled back from the tomb of Jesus, after which it is believed he rose from the dead. Many people believe in these sort of divine miracles.

by science." He argues that science and religion "contradict each other." He claims, "In reality, all such events do have a scientific explanation."[4]

Wonderful and Rare

Not all scientists agree that science and religion contradict each other. In 2004 a poll of medical doctors found that 73 percent of all the doctors believed miracles were possible. Half of the doctors said they had seen miracles happen with their own sick patients. When a rare, unexpected, wonderful thing happens, many religious people believe it is really a miracle. And many people say that miracles have happened to them.

Chapter 2

Healing Miracles

Every year, more than 5 million people still visit the **shrine** built at Lourdes and the spring that Bernadette found in the grotto. Many of them are sick or disabled. They come to bathe in the water and hope for a miracle of healing. In the years since Bernadette's visions, there have been more than 7,000 unexplained healings at Lourdes. The Catholic Church has declared that 67 of them were true miracles.

A Christian Story

One of the miracles happened to John Traynor of Liverpool, England. He was a soldier in World War I and was badly injured by machine-gun fire. He

12

was paralyzed in one arm and both legs and confined to a wheelchair. He also had seizures from a head wound. In 1923 Traynor decided to go on a **pilgrimage** to Lourdes and pray to be healed. Doctors in England had done all they could for him. Traynor stayed at a hospital in Lourdes and visited the shrine with the help of *brancardiers*. They are helpers at Lourdes who assist the sick. They will carry people on stretchers to the waters.

Nine times Traynor bathed in the waters of the grotto. After the last bath, on July 26, he was returned to the hospital where doctors had been caring

Many sick and paralyzed people take pilgrimages to Lourdes, France, every year, believing that the site of Bernadette's vision of the Virgin Mary has healing powers.

for him because he was so weak and sick. Doctors gave him sleeping medicine that night since he was acting strangely and seemed upset. No one suspected that anything had happened. Early the next morning he awoke and jumped out of bed. This is how he described what happened next:

> First, I knelt on the floor to finish the rosary I had been saying. Then I dashed for the door, pushed aside the two *brancardiers* and ran out into the passage and the open air. . . . I may say here that I had not walked since 1915, and my weight was down to 112 pounds.

Faith Healer

Peter Popoff was a faith healer in the 1980s. He could miraculously tell what sicknesses people had and pray for cures. Then magician James Randi showed it was all a hoax. Popoff had a receiver in his ear. His wife secretly radioed information to him about the sick people in his audience. Fake sick people in the audience pretended to be cured. Randi played a tape of the hoax on television. People stopped believing in Popoff. Today he sells miracle spring water on television.

Dr. Marley was outside the door. When he saw the man over whom he had been watching during the pilgrimage, and whose death he had expected, push two brancardiers aside and run out of the ward, he fell back in amazement. Out in the open now, I ran toward the Grotto, which is about two or three hundred yards from the [hospital]. This stretch of ground was graveled then, not paved, and I was barefoot. I ran the whole way to the grotto without getting the least mark or cut on my bare feet. The brancardiers were running after me, but they could not catch up with me. When they reached the grotto, there I was on my knees, still in my night clothes, praying to our Lady and thanking her. All I knew was that I should thank her and the grotto was the place to do it. The brancardiers stood back, afraid to touch me.[5]

Traynor went home to England and lived a long, healthy life. After an investigation, the Catholic Church declared his cure a miracle in 1926. Their report said the cure was "absolutely outside and beyond the forces of nature."[6]

Many Christians say they have had miracle cures, not just visitors to Lourdes. Unexplained cures happen for people of other religions, too. At Lourdes, Catholics say that Mary **intercedes** with God for them. In some other religions, saints are said to intercede with God for a cure.

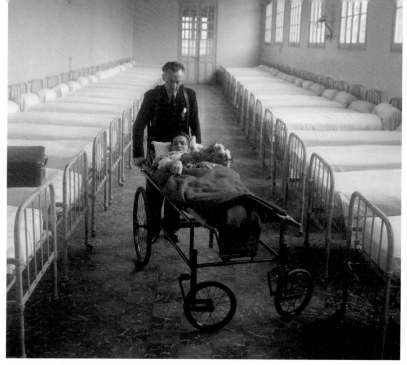

People all over the world have experienced miraculous cures of disease and wounds.

A Jewish Blessing

Shoshana Levin was a Jewish woman who lived in New York. In 1992 her mother was diagnosed with stomach cancer. Levin was desperate. She did not want to lose her mother. She believed that a blessing from Rabbi Menachem Mendel Schneerson would help. People in her sect of Judaism believed the rabbi was a saint. Some even thought he was the Jewish Messiah, or savior. But Schneerson was very old and sick. He had had a bad heart attack and a stroke. He could not walk or talk, but his mind was clear. Secretaries read letters and requests to him, and he would use gestures to tell them what to do.

One morning, Levin went to see a secretary with a letter for Schneerson. It explained about her mother and asked for a blessing. The secretary told Levin to come back that afternoon for an answer and that she and her family should pray, do good deeds, and light candles. The family followed the secretary's instructions. Levin's mother donated money to several charities. The whole family prayed. Levin returned to the secretary's office that afternoon. The secretary said that the rabbi had agreed to give her a blessing. Three days later, Levin's mother went back to the doctor. His tests found no signs of cancer.

Most Jewish people do not believe Schneerson is the Messiah, and many do not believe in miracles. One rabbi says that the true miracle is life itself. But Levin thinks something miraculous happened. Her mother's doctor even said, "Someone's prayers were answered."[7]

Certain Jewish sects believe that Rabbi Menachem Mendel Schneerson (pictured) is a saint and capable of performing miracles.

A Muslim Healing

Muslims often do not believe in miracles either. The story is that the Prophet Muhammad always refused when people asked him to do a miracle. He said the true miracle is the *Koran*, or Muslim holy book. Many Muslims say it is wrong to believe in miracles. Nevertheless, the Sufi sect of Muslims does believe that holy people can perform healing miracles.

Linda Resca is a Sufi spiritual healer in America. Linda Schmitt says that Resca helped her to heal herself from cancer. She says Resca is "blessed with healing presence." Resca worked with Schmitt, praying, meditating, and teaching her to feel God's presence. Six months later, in 2005, Schmitt had medical tests and doctors found her cancer was in remission. Schmitt says, "I very confidently feel that the prayers and counsel of Linda Resca were responsible for this miraculous medical diagnosis."[8]

Praying for God's Help

In four scientific studies of prayer, two showed that sick people got well faster if people prayed for them. Two showed there was no difference between people who were prayed for and people who were not.

An Answer to Hindu Prayers

A painting depicts the Hindu goddess Parvati (left) and Siva. Hindus have long revered the goddess Parvati for her healing powers.

Hindus believe in healing miracles, too. In India a baby girl named Aditi was dying of cholera in the hospital. The doctors could not help her. Kamala, the baby's grandmother, sat with the family by the baby's bed. She prayed to the Hindu god Siva for help. Then she saw an image of a wooden **idol** of the goddess Parvati in her mind. Against doctors' advice, she snatched Aditi up and told the family they were going to the temple at Ochira. It was there that the statue of Parvati stood. She is a healing goddess. The Ochira Temple is like the shrine at Lourdes. Hindus go there to pray to be cured.

Kamala laid Aditi beneath the statue of Parvati and prayed. All the people at the temple saw and helped pray. Kamala cried out, "Amma, Amma, Amma, Amma (Mother, Mother, Mother, Mother!)."[9] Suddenly, Aditi's fever broke. She opened her eyes and lay quietly, breathing easily. She was cured. Everyone agreed it was a miracle, and the family promised to honor the goddess for the rest of their lives.

Chapter 3

Miracle Messages

Not all miracles are cures. Ruksana Patel said she experienced a different kind of miracle in 1996—a message from God.

Allah in a Vegetable

Patel lived in England. One morning she went shopping and bought an aubergine, an eggplant, to cook for supper. She brought the vegetable home and sliced it open. She stared at the seeds in the center and could not believe what she was seeing. The seeds were arranged in a perfect pattern that spelled out the Muslim symbol for "Ya-Allah." It means "Allah exists."

Patel and her husband were thrilled. They took the aubergine to the priest at their mosque. He said

20

the message was a miracle, and many faithful Muslims came to see the vegetable. The priest said, "In all my 30 years as a priest, I have never witnessed anything like this. It is wonderful for the community."[10]

The Hindu Milk Miracle

Messages that seem to come from God are exciting to believers. One of the most famous signs of godly presence is called the Hindu milk miracle. The first sign of a miracle happened in New Delhi, India, just before dawn on September 21, 1995. A worshipper

Hindu devotees crowd around a stone sculpture of the deity Ganesha attempting to have the idol drink milk.

Brains and Pictures

Human brains try to make patterns out of everything. That is why people see a man in the moon and pictures in clouds. It is an illusion called pareidolia. Diana Duyser sold a grilled cheese sandwich on eBay for $28,000. She saw the face of the Virgin Mary on it, and so did lots of eBay bidders.

came to his temple with an offering of milk for the god Ganesha. Ganesha is an elephant-headed god. Hindus often honor their gods with food. The worshipper held a spoonful of milk to the trunk of Ganesha's statue. Then, he said, the milk disappeared from the spoon as Ganesha drank it.

People were in awe, and all over India they hurried to their temples to bring milk to all the idols. As the people held spoons of milk to the statues' lips, they saw the statues drinking it. By noon of that day, Hindu worshippers throughout the world were going to their temples and feeding milk to the gods.

One Indian woman expressed the amazement of many. She is Mabati Kasori. She said, "It's unbelievable. My friends told me about it, and I just thought it was rubbish. But then I did it myself. I swear that the spoon was drained."[11] A businessman named Parmeesh Soti agreed with her. He was sure he had witnessed a miracle. He said, "It cannot be a **hoax**. Where would all that milk go to? It just disappeared in front of my eyes."[12]

How It Might Have Happened

A hoax is a trick designed to fool people. Some people thought the milk miracle was a hoax, but no one could explain how it could happen all over the world. So some scientists looked for a natural explanation for the milk drinking. T. Jayaraman, a scientist in Madras, India, says there is a natural

Some believe that the disappearance of the milk offered to statues of Ganesha is not miraculous, but instead, has a scientific explanation.

reason that the milk disappeared. He explains that liquid in a shallow container (like a spoon) curves a little and sticks together. This is called surface tension. When the liquid is touched to a hard surface (like an idol's lips), the surface tension is broken. Then, the liquid flows out. It flows into any tiny crack in the idol. If the idol is already wet, it flows easily along the surface into the channels of water. The milk is so thinned out that it does not show. The milk does not disappear. It remains in the material of the idol or collects around its base.

Believing, No Matter What

Jayaraman has an explanation for the milk miracle, but not everyone is convinced. Rikee Verma was a journalist in London, England. She believed that the milk drinking was real. She wrote an article in the *Times* and reported:

> Being a religious person, I first went to [my] upstairs bedroom . . . and placed a spoonful of milk against a photograph of Ganesh and was astonished to find within seconds that the spoon was half empty. I checked to make sure that the glass frame of the photograph was not wet. It was dry. . . . This was clearly a message from the gods saying: "We are here, here's the proof."[13]

The Hindu milk miracle stopped as mysteriously as it started. No one knows why the idols stopped drinking their milk, but believers say it was a true miracle. Other religions report miraculous signs, too. Catholics have reported weeping or bleeding statues throughout the world. Sometimes these signs are proved to be hoaxes. Other times, no one knows how they happened.

A Message from Mary

In November 2005 at a small Vietnamese Catholic Church in Sacramento, California, a statue of the Virgin Mary in the church garden began weeping tears of blood. For weeks a red fluid streamed from the statue's eyes. Church members were amazed and came to the statue to pray. One church member, Andre Nguyen, says, "To me, personally, it is a

Try This at Home

T. Jayaraman says to pour a small drop of water on a smooth table. Carefully puncture the bulge of water with a fingertip. Draw a line with the fingertip toward the edge of the table. The water makes a channel. It does not spread out. Now try feeding water on a spoon to a statue. Use a small spoon, and hold it to the corner of the mouth. See if the water channels away.

miracle. You believe it or don't believe it, that's okay. But I strongly believe it."[14]

When others heard about the statue's tears, hundreds came to see for themselves. Some came to pray, and others came to ask for healing miracles or help with other problems. One woman rubbed her forehead with the tears and said her vision got better so she could see to drive at night again. Another visitor

When a statue of the Virgin Mary at a Vietnamese church in Sacramento, California, was seen with red stains coming from her eyes, many took this as a sign from God.

was Dave Leatherby. He did not ask for healing, but he did believe the statue's tears were a real miracle. He said: "Just the fact that it's coming from the eyes and it's a red color like blood, I would say that there's a miracle either way. Even if there's a natural explanation, it's a sign. . . . I think many people have forgotten about God, and I think she's weeping about God's children who are lost and are searching and looking for answers."[15]

Suspicious Miracles

The Catholic Church is not ready to call the weeping statue a miracle for sure. Sacramento priest Father James Murphy explains, "These kind of phenomena are fairly common. But the number that turn out to be miraculous are very, very rare."[16] The church would have to conduct a careful investigation before deciding that the weeping statue was a miracle. That is because sometimes so-called miracles are really hoaxes.

One priest in Australia removed a weeping statue from his church because he believed the weeping was not real. When the statue was tested, scientists discovered that the tears were actually made of vegetable oil. They could not say exactly how the oil got into the statue, but they thought the tears were faked.

At a Vietnamese church in Australia in 2004, another Virgin Mary statue was weeping. The bishop took the statue to a scientist for testing. The

Some churches have discovered that weeping statues are hoaxes that are caused by placing oil or other liquids in the statue to make it look like it is crying.

chemist found two tiny holes drilled through the statue's head. He found that rose-scented oil made up the "tears." Most likely someone was trying to fool faithful believers. The bishop, John Bathersby, said, "I must declare that what has happened . . . cannot be said to be of supernatural origin."[17]

Some signs can be scientifically tested to see if they are hoaxes. But some miracles just have to be believed.

28 Miracles

Chapter 4

Miracles of Survival

Virgil Craft lived a long, active life until he died in 1999 at the age of 84, and he always said his life was a miracle. Only because of a series of miraculous events did he live to grow old.

How It Started

Craft was 36 years old and lived in Wise County, Virginia, where he worked for a coal company. One Saturday in 1951 he and a crew were loading coal into railroad cars so it could be shipped out of town. Craft was working alone at the top end of the hollow, getting two empty coal cars to roll down the grade to the men who were loading coal at the bottom. He did what he always did. The two cars

Is This a Good Argument?

Philip Pecorino is a professor. He says: "If surviving an auto accident were to be considered a miracle because GOD brought it about then so would DEATH be a miracle because if GOD determines who survives such an accident so too does GOD determine who dies! However, we do not hear people say: He died in the accident! It was a miracle!"

Philip A. Pecorino, "Miracles," *Philosophy of Religion*, online textbook, Queensborough Community College, 2001. www2.sunysuffolk.edu/pecorip/SCCCWEB/ETEXTS/PHIL_of_RELIGION_TEXT/CHAPTER_5_ARGUMENTS_EXPERIENCE/Miracles.htm.

were hooked together. He pushed them forward, got them rolling, and hopped aboard the front car for the ride down the track.

As the cars picked up speed, Craft suddenly realized that the front car had no brakes. He was racing downward and had no way to warn the men below of the danger. Desperately, Craft tried to leap across the coal bin in the center and reach the hand brake on the other end of the open car. Just as he jumped and grabbed the brake, the rear car slammed into his car, knocking Craft over the side. Blindly, he groped for a handhold as he fell. His hand grasped a rod on the outside of the car, and he used his grip to keep himself from sliding under the cars onto the tracks. But his legs twisted under the cars. Eight wheels ran over his legs.

Death Seemed Close

Thankfully, the accident happened in front of the little office about halfway down the grade. Craft's supervisor witnessed the horrible accident and came running out. Craft's legs were mangled, and

Many people believe that the power of prayer through vigils can heal the sick and wounded.

he was bleeding terribly. The supervisor quickly clamped one hand over an artery that was spurting blood. "Frank," said Craft, "Don't move your hand. You've got my life in your hands."[18]

At that time, there were no rescue squads or helicopter flights to major hospitals. The funeral home responded to calls for help and drove people to the nearest hospital in a special hearse/ambulance. One of the workmen made a frantic telephone call to the funeral home. Lewis Estes, who worked there, came as fast as he could. Estes and the crew got Craft loaded into the ambulance.

At the local hospital the doctor took one look at Craft's injuries and decided there was nothing he could do. Craft's injuries were too severe. So Estes loaded Craft back into his ambulance and drove on to the next hospital. He tore along the narrow, twisting mountain road at speeds of 100 miles an hour (161km/hour). In one hairpin turn he slid sideways from the high speed. Even Craft was afraid they would wreck, but Estes regained control and sped on.

Help from Many Places

Finally, he got Craft to the hospital in the little town of Norton. The hospital was small, but it had a doctor who could help. He had been a military surgeon and had recently moved to Norton. He had operated on war-wounded men, but he later said Craft's wound was the worst he had ever seen.

Besides, Craft had lost too much blood, and the hospital did not have any stored blood. The surgeon could not operate without blood transfusions.

The surgeon called the local radio station and asked the disc jockey to put out a call for blood donations. Of the first twenty people who responded to the plea, eighteen had Craft's blood type, which was O+. (In America, 38 percent of people have that blood type.) The doctor had to amputate Craft's legs to save his life. He was not sure Craft could survive the operation, but he would try.

The surgery lasted about four hours. Word spread throughout the community that Craft was in terrible danger. Several churches held prayer **vigils** until they got word that the operation was over. Craft survived. Later he said, "God watched over me. It wasn't my time to die."[19] The surgeon said to Craft, "I didn't save your life. I was just an instrument."[20]

Miracles with a Reason

Craft not only survived, he went home strong and healthy. His legs were gone, but that did not stop him from leading an active life. His son remembers hearing his father tell the amazing story and explaining why it was a series of miracles. His son recalls: "It was a miracle he wasn't killed outright in the accident; a miracle he didn't bleed to death; a miracle the ambulance didn't wreck; a miracle that the first eighteen people matched his blood type; a miracle this doctor had just moved to Norton."[21]

Believing that God had spared his life by a divine miracle so he could help others, Virgil Craft started a blood bank in his town.

All his life, Craft credited his survival to a miracle from God. He began a campaign to get a blood bank for the town of Norton. The campaign was successful, and the blood bank saved the lives of mountain citizens for decades. Craft believed that was why he had survived—God wanted him to start a blood bank for Norton and gave him a miracle so he could do it.

A 9/11 Miracle

Stanley Praimnath knows he owes his life to a miracle, too. On September 11, 2001, he survived the terrorist attack on the World Trade Center in New York City. When the hijacked plane hit, Praimnath was at his desk on the 81st floor of the south tower. He remembered later: "All I can see is this big gray plane, with red letters on the wing and on the tail, bearing down on me. But this thing is happening in slow motion. The plane appeared to be like 100 yards away. I said, 'Lord, you take control, I can't help myself here.'"[22]

Praimnath hid under his desk as the plane crashed into the building. It seemed a miracle that he was unhurt. He could see a plane wing not 50 feet (15m) away, and piles of debris lay all around him. He was frightened and felt completely helpless. So he prayed, and suddenly, he says, "God gave me so much power in my body that I was able to shake everything off."[23]

They All Survived

Air France Flight 358 crashed and burst into flames at the Toronto, Canada, airport on August 2, 2005. Many news reports said it was a miracle that 100 percent of the passengers survived. Almost 300 people were quickly evacuated from the burning plane by the skillful and brave flight crew. Was it a survival miracle or a fortunate event, aided by well-trained people?

He crawled over the rubble, looking for a way to escape. Then, he saw a light in the distance. It was a flashlight carried by Brian Clark, a survivor from the 84th floor, working his way down the emergency stairs. Praimnath, however, could not reach the stairs. A wall stood in the way. Desperately, both men punched at the wall until they had made a hole big enough for Praimnath to crawl through.

Together, the men leaned on each other and slowly climbed down the 80 flights of stairs. At the bottom they encountered a sea of flames. Praimnath said to Clark, "You're going to have to soak yourself under the sprinklers. The only way out is through the fire."[24] The two men drenched themselves and ran through the flaming door and out into the street. They ran to the nearby Trinity Church, and as Praimnath grasped the gate, he saw the south tower collapse.

In God's Hands

Praimnath was the only person to survive from the 81st floor. In a *700 Club* interview, he said:

> Three miracles, one day. . . . I asked the Lord to take over. I couldn't do this. He pushed that plane away from me. I asked Him to send somebody, anybody, to help me, and He sent Brian Clark to help me. And He knew I had to get to safety before He let go of the building. And as soon as I held on to His house, the church gate, the building col-

Though thousands died in the September 11, 2001, terrorist attacks on the World Trade Center, Stanley Praimnath is sure he survived because of a miracle after praying to God to help him.

lapsed because He's still doing miracles in people's lives today."[25]

People like Praimnath do not have doubts. They believe in miracles. No proof is necessary. Miracles and faith go together.

Notes

Chapter 1: Do You Believe in Miracles?

1. Quoted in Catholic Pilgrims.com, "Apparitions at Lourdes." www.catholicpilgrims.com/lourdes/bd_lourdes_apparitions.htm.
2. Quoted in Catholic Pilgrims.com, "I Am the Immaculate Conception." www.catholicpilgrims.com/lourdes/bg_lourdes_conception.htm.
3. Quoted in Catholic Pilgrims.com, "Investigation of the Apparitions at Lourdes." www.catholicpilgrims.com/lourdes/bh_investigation.htm.
4. P.M. Bhargava, "Preface," in *Science Versus Miracles*, by B. Premanand. Reprinted online at Indian Skeptic Pages. www.indian-skeptic.org/html/svm3.htm.

Chapter 2: Healing Miracles

5. Quoted in Our Lady of the Rose Library, "Miracles of Lourdes." www.olrl.org/stories/lourdes.shtml.
6. Quoted in Our Lady of the Rose Library, "Miracles of Lourdes."
7. Quoted in Kenneth L. Woodward, "What Miracles

Mean," *Newsweek*, May 1, 2000. www.rickross. com/reference/general/general240.html.

8. Linda Schmitt, "A Healing Story: 'A Medical Miracle,'" University of Spiritual Healing and Sufism. www.sufiuniversity.org/Reading/healing _story.php.

9. Quoted in *Hinduism Today*, "Puja's Passion," book review, November 1999. www.hinduism today.com/archives/1999/11/1999-11-10. shtml.

Chapter 3: Miracle Messages

10. Quoted in The Miracles Page, "Signs of Allah: Miraculous Aubergine (1996)." www.mcn.org /1/Miracles/Allah2.html.

11. Quoted in *Asheville Magazine*, "Hindu Milk Miracle." www.newfrontier.com/asheville/ hindu-milk-miracle.htm.

12. Quoted in *Asheville Magazine*, "Hindu Milk Miracle."

13. Quoted in *Asheville Magazine*, "Hindu Milk Miracle."

14. Quoted in Marcy Valenzuela, "Tears of Blood Appear on Virgin Mary Statue," CBS5.com, November 21, 2005. http://cbs5.com/top stories/local_story_326014939.html.

15. Quoted in CBS13.com, "Sacramento's Crying Virgin Mary on *CBS Early Show*," November 29, 2005. http://cbs13.com/virginmary/local _story_333113220.html.

16. Quoted in CBS13.com, "Sacramento's Crying Virgin Mary on CBS *Early Show*."

17. Quoted in B.A. Robinson, "Church Artifacts with Miraculous Powers: Weeping/Bleeding Statues," Religious Tolerance.org, August 2, 2004. www.religioustolerance.org/chr_stat.htm.

Chapter 4: Miracles of Survival

18. Curtis Craft, interview with the author, Dundas, VA, October, 2007.

19. Curtis Craft, interview.

20. Quoted in Craft, interview.

21. Quoted in Craft, interview.

22. Quoted in American Tribute, "Survivor Stories." http://jeanne_and_trev.tripod.com/america/id17.html.

23. Quoted in John W. Kennedy, John Cockroft, and Peter K. Johnson, "Plucked from the Fire," Stanley Praimanth.com. www.stanley praimnath.com/1.htm.

24. Quoted in Kennedy, Cockroft, and Johnson, "Plucked from the Fire."

25. Quoted in *700 Club*, "Saved Miraculously from Under the Wing," Stanley Praimanth.com. www.stanleypraimnath.com/1.htm.

Glossary

hallucinations: Things seen, heard, or felt that are not part of reality; usually experienced because of a mental illness or a drug.

hoax: An act meant to trick or cheat.

idol: An image made to represent a god and used as an object of worship.

illusion: A false experience created in the mind; a dream or vision that seems real but is not.

intercedes: Prays to God for another person.

pilgrimage: A religious journey to a sacred place.

shrine: A place of worship and religious devotion.

skeptics: Doubters. Those who are suspicious of or question accepted beliefs.

vigils: Religious watches for a special purpose.

For Further Exploration

Books

Joy Barrow, *Sikhism*. North Vancouver, Canada: Walrus/Whitecap, 2005. This book examines what it is like to be a Sikh.

Alan Brown, *Christianity*. North Vancouver, Canada: Walrus/Whitecap, 2005. This book examines what it is like to be a Christian.

Ian Graham, *Judaism*. North Vancouver, Canada: Walrus/Whitecap, 2005. This book examines what it is like to be a Jew.

Claire Llewellyn, *Saints and Angels*. Boston: Kingfisher, 2003. With beautiful artwork, this book describes the lives and works of Christian saints and the angels whom some Christians believe watch over people. Bernadette Soubirous's story is included.

Kerena Marchant, *Muhammad and Islam*. London: Hodder Wayland, 2005. This book describes the life of the Prophet Muhammad, the founder of Islam, and the important ideas that he taught.

Ranchor Prime, *Hinduism*. North Vancouver, Canada: Walrus/Whitecap, 2005. This book looks at Hindu experiences.

Jan Thompson, *Islam*. North Vancouver, Canada: Walrus/Whitecap, 2005. This book examines the Muslim religion.

Mel Thompson, *Buddhism*. North Vancouver, Canada: Walrus/Whitecap, 2005. This book examines what Buddhists believe.

Web Sites

Joan Wester Anderson (www.joanwanderson. com/index.htm). Anderson is an author who has written several books about miracles, angels, and other wonders. Visitors can click on her Archives link for a long list of accounts of children who have experienced miracles.

Miracle, The Sacred White Buffalo (www.home stead.com/WhiteBuffaloMiracle/). In Native American religious belief, a white buffalo is a sacred miracle and a symbol from the spirits. Visitors to this site can learn about a white buffalo named Miracle, born on a Wisconsin farm in 1994, and revered by many people throughout her life. There is also a link to read about Miracle's white calf, born in 2006.

Miracle or Not? From Philip A. Pecorino, *Philosophy of Religion*, online textbook, Queensborough Community College, 2001. (www2.sunysuffolk. edu/pecorip/SCCCWEB/ETEXTS/PHIL_of_ RELIGION_TEXT/CHAPTER_5_ARGU MENTS_EXPERIENCE/Miracles-or-not.htm).

This page is from a text for college students, but it has many pictures of events and objects that have been called miracles. The author says people should look at the photos and decide for themselves.

United Religions Initiative Kids (www.uri. org/kids/). Visitors to this site can use the links to learn the basic beliefs of many different religions.

Index

45

Picture Credits

About the Author

Toney Allman holds degrees from Ohio State University and University of Hawaii. She currently lives in rural Virginia, where she enjoys exploring the world by writing books for students.